by John Guyatt

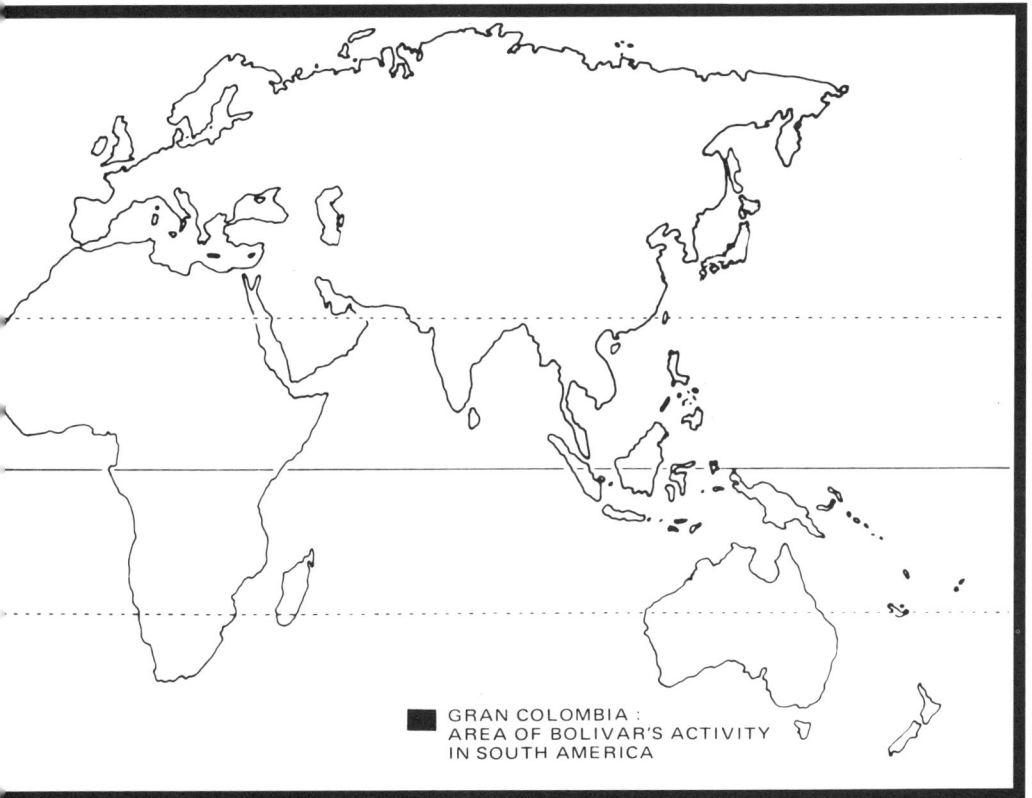

GRAN COLOMBIA :
AREA OF BOLIVAR'S ACTIVITY
IN SOUTH AMERICA

Greenhaven Press, Inc.

P.O. BOX 289009
SAN DIEGO, CA 92198-0009

A map of South America showing the capital cities and main physical relief. The North West corner shows the three states, Colombia, Venezuela and Ecuador, that formed Gran Colombia.

A view of Caracas, the capital of Venezuela

EARLY LIFE

Simon Bolivar was born in Caracas in 1783. His father was rich and owned a great deal of land but died while Simon was only a small child. His mother died too when he was a boy so that other people had to bring him up. He was not very well-behaved, was untidy and seems to have been a difficult child. The job of looking after him fell largely on his black nurse. Years later he said, 'I never knew any father but her.'

He was intelligent, but disliked being forced to work. In fact, he even threw ink at his teachers. Luckily the tutor he liked best didn't try to make him learn everything, but only what interested him. Because of this, Bolivar always enjoyed reading although other people were sometimes surprised at the things he had never learnt! As a boy, Bolivar liked games and riding more than studying. He grew up to be rather a short man but also very strong: this early toughening was to help him greatly during later fighting.

Spanish settler in the New World in the early nineteenth century

CARACAS IN THE 1780s

What sort of a country did Bolivar grow up in? Caracas, where he lived, was the chief town of the province of New Grenada, made up of today's Colombia and Venezuela This province formed part of the huge Spanish Empire in Central and South America, ruled from across the ocean by Spain. It had been built over two centuries before and was no longer a raw frontier town. Spanish ships crossed the Atlantic between Venezuela and Spain and most of the expensive things to be bought in Madrid could also be found in Caracas. Only a few could buy these luxuries. These people were the white, upper class wealthy families, called *Creoles* throughout Latin America. Most of the time they lived in the big towns or ports on the coast, although they also owned big farms inland. In fact, the white upper classes born in Venezuela were much more similar

A caste. This girl's ancestry is probably a combination of mulatto and South American Indian

A South American Indian

to the Spanish over the ocean than to the majority of their fellow countrymen.

As the young Bolivar travelled out to his family's farms, he would have noticed many changes from the life he knew in his parents' house. Away from the wealthy districts of Caracas, the streets would be filled with much poorer coloured people, or *Castes,* whose parents were a mixture of black slaves, whites and Indians. (D1)* These Castes in the towns were ambitious. They hated the white upper classes who in turn tried to keep them in their place. As Bolivar left the town, the people would again change and the fields would be filled with Indian peasants, the most down-trodden people of all in Latin America. (D2) Most of the time they suffered in silence, but if pushed too far they would rebel. (D3)

Beyond the neat farms in the valleys near the sea lay the jungle, and beyond it towered the Andes mountains. Even after two centuries of Spanish conquest, few people had pushed that far inland. If you wanted to visit another part of Latin America, it was quickest to go by sea, since few places were far from the coast and very few roads crossed the continent. Not even all the coast was explored or controlled by the Spanish Government. For instance there was a large part of the Venezuelan coast which only wild and savage cowboys knew well. Much of Venezuela and most of its people were thus strange to the young Bolivar and most of his class. Strange and distrusted: later he was to have to learn about them.

*The reference (D) indicates the numbered documents at the end of this book. 5

BOLIVAR'S VISIT TO EUROPE

As a teenager and a young man Bolivar went to Europe a number of times. These visits excited him very much. Caracas must have seemed to him a very dead and boring place as he visited Spain, France and Italy. In Madrid he visited the royal court, fell violently in love with the daughter of a Spanish nobleman, and married her in 1802. In Paris he saw the great Napoleon at the height of his success. He was impressed by Napoleon's popularity amongst the French but sickened by his pride. Later on other people were to feel the same way about Bolivar himself.

During his early visits, Bolivar had no idea that he was to become the Liberator of Latin America. When he married he returned to Venezuela with his wife to settle down to farming his lands. However, his wife died of fever within nine months and Bolivar returned to Europe to try to forget his sorrow. This was to be the turning point in his life. The ideas of freedom, which had not

The rounding up of cattle on the plains of Venezuela

A farmyard in Colombia

greatly concerned him when he heard of them before, now began to arouse his passionate interest. He visited Rome and all that he had read about ancient Rome came alive to him. The Romans were never slaves to anyone and thought their freedom one of the most important things in the world. Why, Bolivar thought, should Latin Americans not be free? Why should they go on taking orders from Spain? Why should they not govern themselves? Perhaps, too, he wanted the fame of being the man to free his country. (D4—5)

SPAIN AND HER COLONIES

When he arrived back in Caracas, Bolivar found trouble already brewing. For some years Britain and Spain had been at war, and the British Navy had cut sea communications between Spain and her American colonies. Until then, the Spanish government in Madrid had tried to run Latin America without taking much notice of what the people there wanted. All the jobs in the government in Latin America were held by people born in Spain. (D6) This, naturally, was disliked very much by the Creoles who wanted a share in running their country. With messages and instructions from Madrid dwindling to a trickle, the Creoles found themselves having to take more control.

Before the war, too, Spain had tried to keep all the trade with Latin America to herself, and had banned other European countries from selling their goods there.(D7) Since French, Dutch and British

Bolivar as a young man

goods were usually much cheaper, a flourishing smuggling business had developed on the side. (D8–9) With the war and the Spanish Navy in trouble, British ships quite openly sold their cargoes wherever they wanted. The local people obviously liked this since the prices were much lower.

The upper class Creoles did well out of the war, therefore. They had greater power and could buy more for their money. But the majority of them did not want to break away from Spain altogether. Why? Firstly, as we have seen, a Creole in Caracas felt much closer to a Spaniard across the Atlantic than to a rough cowboy from his own country. There were, even so, differences between Creoles and Spaniards. These differences were rather like those, say, between Australians, Canadians and Englishmen. Secondly, the Creoles were very frightened of what might happen if fighting broke out in Latin America. If the Creoles and the Spaniards began fighting one another, wouldn't the Castes and the Indians see their chance to rebel? Only if the white rulers, whether Spanish or Creole, stuck together could the non-whites be kept in their place. In Mexico and Cuba, the Spaniards and Creoles did in fact stick together for just this reason.

Probably most Creoles wanted things to stay much as they were during the war — that is, still part of the Spanish Empire but with much greater freedom within it. What was it, then, that pushed Bolivar and others into fighting for a complete break with Spain? Firstly, the Spanish government made it clear that when peace came again, it would try to put back the old controls. In other words, Spain was not interested in meeting the Creoles half way: it was all or nothing. Secondly, there had already been the great example of North America. There the thirteen British colonies had fought the American War of Independence for their freedom and now seemed to be a proud,

free and successful nation *(The American Revolution)*. Why should the Latin Americans settle for less than the North Americans? Even more recently the French had had a great revolution against their king, hoping for greater freedom for the French people. Bolivar and others had visited Europe and had been excited by these events. Thirdly, as we will see, the violence and the savagery of the fighting once started made it very difficult for people to

Napoleon in his coronation robes. This picture shows him as a very proud, regal and awe-inspiring figure.

*Titles in brackets refer to other booklets in the Program

avoid taking sides — either completely pro-Spanish or completely anti. To stand in the middle became impossible.

THE BEGINNING OF THE FIGHTING

The spark that began the revolution came in 1808 when Napoleon made his brother Joseph King of Spain and dethroned the true Spanish king. The Spanish people and the Creoles would not obey their new 'king', and Spain now became Britain's ally. In Latin America 'Committees' of the most important citizens were set up to support the true king. However, as the French tightened their grip on Spain, the power of the real king dwindled to nothing.

Some Creoles felt the time had come for a complete break with Spain; others wanted to stay loyal. In the wars that were to follow the Creoles were going to fight one another as well as the Spanish. It was a civil war as well as a war of independence.

THE FIRST CAMPAIGN: THE MIRANDA INCIDENT

A special meeting was soon called by many Creoles to declare Venezuela independent. All over Latin America the same thing happened, especially in the South, which is today's Chile and Argentina. Although parts of Venezuela wouldn't join the rebellion the chances of success seemed good. Above all, in 1810 Francisco de Miranda had returned. Since a young man he had wanted Venezuela to break

away from Spain, and he had had to live in England as an exile. He was now into his sixties but was immediately put in charge of the rebel army.

The first blow to the rebels was a violent earthquake which destroyed most of rebel-held Caracas. To many people it seemed like God's punishment for the rebels.

Next, Miranda showed that he didn't understand how the Spanish army could be beaten. The Spanish were trained to fight set-piece battles as in Europe. They were used to armies marching in regular lines and meeting on a battlefield where each side would batter away until one side was beaten. The way to win this sort of war was to have a bigger army than your enemy and to have it very well trained. Miranda's army, however, wasn't very big and most of its soldiers had only joined up a few months before. The rebels' advantage lay in the fact that they had a far better knowledge of the countryside. They could take short cuts across open country, jungles or hills, while the Spaniards stuck to the roads. Since they carried less equipment than the Spanish they could travel much more quickly, and seem to be in more places at once than the bigger but clumsier Spanish army. Under Bolivar they were going to win by using these guerilla methods. Miranda, however, tried to fight the Spanish along the old lines.

After a little fighting Miranda lost his nerve and surrendered. Bolivar found Miranda trying to leave the country and turned him over to the Spanish. In return the

Spanish let Bolivar leave the country as a free man. Miranda, however, was sent to dungeons in Spain where he later died. It is difficult to know the truth about this incident, but it is very possible that Bolivar had seen a wonderful chance to get rid of Miranda so that he, Bolivar, could take over as leader.

BOLIVAR TAKES COMMAND: GUERILLA WARFARE BEGINS

Bolivar escaped, but soon he was back in Colombia planning to cross into Venezuela. He had only six hundred men and five cannon while the Spaniards had many times more. However, Bolivar moved so quickly that the Spanish forces stationed all over the country didn't have time to join together. They were caught in small groups and surprised. In ninety days, Bolivar's rebels crossed eight hundred miles of rough countryside, smashed five Spanish units, captured fifty cannon and three ammunition dumps, and arrived in Caracas in triumph. Very impressed with Bolivar's success, the Venezuelans gave him every power to rule the country. But his triumph wasn't going to last long.

The fighting had already become very savage and both sides used much cruelty and terror. Bolivar had in this campaign ordered a war to the death — which meant that all armed Spanish soldiers taken prisoner were to be shot. Bolivar said that this was to repay the Spanish who also shot the rebels if they caught them. (D10) The

Francisco de Miranda as he was in his 60's when he returned to lead the rebel army.

effect was to increase the cruelty on both sides, and Bolivar reversed the order some years later. (D11)

Bolivar now made one of his few mistakes. Some of the Spanish forces hadn't yet been destroyed, but instead of going after them before they had time to band together, Bolivar stayed in Caracas. Also, Napoleon had been defeated and Spain was now free to send more troops to America. Thousands of extra soldiers were on their way to crush the rebels. Most important of all, the Spanish were getting the support of the cowboys of the plains.

These cowboys despised white people — who in turn were afraid

11

of them. They didn't care or understand much about the struggle going on amongst the whites, but they were very interested in money, and the Spanish paid them to fight on their side. This really meant the end for Bolivar, because these cowboys were some of the best horsemen in America. In a short time, bands of looting and butchering cowboys were approaching Caracas. Nearly all of Bolivar's troops were wiped out and in 1814 he had again to flee the country.

THE ORINOCO CAMPAIGN

The next few years were an uphill struggle for Bolivar. From Jamaica he planned another expedition to free his country. Bolivar chose the delta region of the Orinoco river for his new base, and established his headquarters there in 1817. It was an area of thick jungle and swamps where Spanish troops would find it difficult to move but where the rebels would know their way. What was really important was that the plains of the cowboys lay near by.

Bolivar knew that his earlier enemies had to be won over to the rebels' side. He needed the cowboys because only their numbers and skills could drive out the Spanish. Some of Bolivar's officers didn't like the idea of bringing in non-whites. Bolivar, however, said that the battle against Spain was to be

'Lo Mismo (The Same)' *from* 'The Disasters of War' *by Goya. This picture shows the cruelty that must have occured when Bolivar gave his 'no prisoners' order.*

The cowboys riding across the plains

fought by *all* Venezuelans. In fact, since he was a young man he had shown far less colour prejudice than most of his class. He had already promised black slaves their freedom if they fought for him. Now he turned to the cowboys. To them and their leader, José Paez, he could offer some money from his own fortune. (Bolivar was born into a rich family; by the time he died he had spent nearly everything in the cause of freedom.) Even more than money Paez admired Bolivar as a person. His courage, his toughness and his success as a soldier pleased Paez. In quite a short time the cowboy bands had changed sides and fought alongside Bolivar.

Bolivar knew that he could use guerilla methods to wear down the Spaniards. By moving secretly and quickly through the countryside, he could tie down even the massive Spanish army with a small number of men. He also knew that the hard core of the Spanish army would have to be wiped out in battle. Unlike Miranda, he saw these battles as the final blows to an army already weakened by guerilla campaigns. The final battles would need some trained soldiers to stand up to the disciplined Spanish troops. As if to answer his wants, about 4,000 volunteer soldiers came to Venezuela from Europe. Many of these were British soldiers from the Napoleonic wars looking for new adventures. These were to be as important as the cowboys.

Britain helped the rebels in another way, too. She had begun to sell more goods to Latin

*Jose Antonio Paez, the cowboy
leader, who admired Bolivar and
joined him to fight against
the Spanish*

America than ever before, and she
did not want the old controls on
trade put back. If Latin America
became free, then she could go on
selling more and more there.
Britain therefore warned other
European countries that she
would not let them help Spain
regain her Empire by sending their
troops to Latin America.

CROSSING THE ANDES

The tide turned when Bolivar
planned an amazing and daring
raid across the Andes mountains
into the next door province of
Colombia. He planned to link up
with the Colombian rebels to catch
the Spanish by surprise. He knew
that the Spanish — and most
people — thought it impossible to
cross the Andes with an army.

Starting with 2,000 troops,
including British volunteers and
cowboys, he marched inland from
the coast. Ahead lay 1,000 miles
of jungle and mountains. It was
the rainy season and streams that
normally could be crossed on foot
were now raging torrents. Rafts
had to be built. For a week the
army waded through the flooded
countryside with water often up
to their waists. Slowly they left
the jungle behind them as they
climbed the foothills of the Andes.

*A portrait of Bolivar when he was
42*

The dense jungle that Bolivar's troops had to cross before reaching the Andes

A panoramic view of the Andes from a sketch made in 1873

The Calle Real, the principal street in Bogota

It was open grasslands now, and when it didn't rain there was no shade from the burning sun. This heat was followed by the bitter cold of the mountain passes. (D12) Frost-bitten and staggering through the biting wind and snow, the survivors finally reached Colombia. All the horses and pack animals had been lost, and Bolivar's men had little more than their clothes and their muskets. The local people, however, welcomed them, fed them, helped them get their strength back and found fresh horses for the cowboys.

CAPTURING BOGOTA

Bolivar's aim was to capture Bogota, the capital of Colombia. A strong Spanish force stood in the way and had to be defeated. This Bolivar did at the very important battle of Boyaca on August 7th, 1819.

The Spanish troops were pulling back and Bolivar knew that the Spanish would have to cross a bridge over a small river at a place named Boyaca. When the Spanish commander reached this bridge, he let his men sprawl out on the ground for their midday meal. Because he had so many more men than the rebels, he thought he was bound to win the battle, and became careless.

The rebels crept up slowly through the undergrowth, without being noticed by the Spanish. Meanwhile the cowboys had found a crossing place further down the river and were coming up behind the Spanish. Suddenly, with the British volunteers leading the

Jose de San Martin, who had successfully led the rebel armies in Chile and Argentina

attack from the front, the rebels charged. Caught in the open, dozy from the midday sun and food, the large Spanish army was shattered in a short time. The road to Bogota was now open.

In the next few years Bolivar beat Spanish armies in Venezuela and Peru. Under his leadership the northern part of Latin America had been freed. It seemed to be a time of triumph, but the shadows were gathering around.

MEETING WITH SAN MARTIN

While Bolivar had been fighting in the north, the rebels in Argentina and Chile in the South had been led by another great hero, José de San Martin. He too had taken an army across the Andes and caught the Spanish forces by surprise. He had then made his way up towards Peru. In 1822, just before the final Spanish defeat, these two great men met in Ecuador. They were very different people. On the surface they were friendly to each other, but underneath they were suspicious. Each thought that the other was too ambitious. Bolivar thought that San Martin wanted to become King of Peru. (D13) People were later to say that Bolivar himself wanted to be a king . . . They could not work together and San Martin realised that if one of them did not give way there would be trouble. It is a sign of San Martin's greatness that he put Latin America before his own ambition: he resigned his command and left for Europe.

THE PROBLEMS OF PEACE

Many people in South America hoped that they would become strong and rich, as the North Americans had after their war of independence from Britain. Why did this not happen?

Bolivar had never wanted to be just a soldier, and his army expected him to form a new government. His dream was to unite the three parts of New Grenada (now Colombia, Venezuela and Ecuador) into a new country, Gran Colombia. Although the Spanish had lumped these together, they were separated by mountains and jungles from one another. Their people knew little about the other parts. Bolivar wanted a strong central government to weld them together. Local feelings and the ambitions of the local leaders were to prevent this.

In Venezuela, Paez, the cowboy leader, was plotting to set up his own government. In Colombia and Ecuador, too, men were planning to break up Gran Colombia. Because of the wars, power now was in the hands of the army leaders, and few wanted to give it up. At the same time 'constitutions' were being written by Creoles. These were sets of rules about how governments were to be chosen and how they should work. However, the Creoles did not know much about governing and they did not face up to the problems brought about by the wars. As a result most of the generals took no notice of the constitutions at all. Bolivar would have liked Latin America to be governed by proper rules, but he soon saw that the generals wouldn't obey them. More and more he felt convinced that only really strong dictatorships could hold Latin America together. His rivals said that Bolivar wanted to be king or dictator himself. It is true that as he grew older Bolivar wanted obedience, but he was also thinking of what was best for Latin America.

At the same time that Gran Colombia was beginning to fall apart, Bolivar was planning the Panama Congress, a meeting of the newly independent countries of Latin America, which took place in 1826. He wanted them to form a joint army and navy, and, in time, a kind of United States of Latin America. The meeting was a failure because not all the new countries attended, and those that did disagreed. Another of Bolivar's dreams had come to nothing.

Bitter at the failure of his ideas and weak from years of overwork, Bolivar resigned from the leadership of Gran Colombia. An attempt had been made to kill him, and soon Ecuador and Venezuela broke from Colombia. Bolivar, now very sick, spent his last days on the Colombian coast where he died in 1829. He was only 46. In ten years his triumph had turned into failure.

'THE SOLE BENEFIT'

What had been achieved? Bolivar himself said shortly before he died, 'Independence is the sole benefit we have gained, at the sacrifice of all others.' In place of a badly run and disliked Spanish government, the Latin Americans now ruled themselves. On paper they freely chose their own governments; in practice, faced with chaos and economic ruin, they began a long period of rule by army leaders. (D14) These men were often worse than the old Spanish government, and nearly always far crueller. The Latin Americans were now able to buy and sell with the world as they wished, and the early leaders hoped that their countries would quickly grow rich like the United States. But Britain and the United States were already much richer than Latin America, and could make things more cheaply than she could. This meant that Latin America had to buy British and American factory-made goods, (D15) and sell them raw materials in return. Instead of being tied to

Bolivar in 1829, the year of his death

Spain, she was now tied to even more powerful economic masters. Many Latin American countries were in a terrible state because of the wars and desperately needed to borrow money to keep going at all. The money was provided mainly by the British, and soon Latin America owed money to Europe and America — as it still does today. During the rest of the nineteenth century many countries were so short of money that they sold off their farms and mines to foreigners. For instance Chilean copper mines were mainly bought up by the British. By 1900 it was clear that even if a country flew its own flag, had its own army and government, it could still be

A typical South American slum

A comparison of these two pictures shows how extreme is the contrast of wealth and poverty in today's Latin America

controlled by outsiders if its economy were owned by foreigners.

Despite the fears of many Creoles, the whites remained in power almost everywhere. It is true that slavery was abolished except in Brazil and Cuba, and that everyone was supposed to be free, but, in practice, the right to take part in politics was limited to those who could read and write, which kept out all Indians and

nearly all Castes. By and large it was the Creoles who had gained most from the new freedom. A few non-Creole leaders like Paez were able to become powerful in the chaos of the wars, but such men were few. In the towns the Castes probably found it rather easier to get on in life, but in the countryside the conditions of the Indians deteriorated. (D16–17) This was because the Spanish government had previously let

Bogota, the capital of Colombia

the Indians keep some of their village lands, but now the new governments often passed laws to help Creoles get hold of these Indian lands.

In place of Bolivar's dream of unity based on a shared language, religion and history, the Spanish Empire split up into twenty or so republics. Later many of these were to become rivals and even fight one another. In the hundred and fifty years or so since independence the situation has changed little. There have been peasant revolutions in Mexico, Bolivia and Cuba but on the whole the condition of the Indians has hardly improved. In many of the countries the descendants of the Creoles, joined by an increasing number of Castes, live comfortable lives in the big cities on the coast. Wealth is still mostly made from the export of raw materials, although there are now more industries than there used to be. Often, too, wealth is still based on land owning. In the countryside the old ways have hardly altered. There has been political independence for a long time, but economic progress and a decent life for the majority of the population are as far away as they were when Bolivar died.

DOCUMENT 1

THE CONDITION OF THE CASTES   *MANUEL ABAD Y QUEIPO*
(1751 - 1825) – Spanish priest who served in Latin America

The castes that are descendants of Negro slaves are held inferior even by law. Since tribute is rigorously collected from them without exception, paying tribute has become an indelible brand of their slavery, which cannot be erased by time or the mixing of blood, no matter how many generations have passed. There are many persons among the castes who could be classified as Spaniards by their colour, appearance, and good conduct. This prejudice, however, prevents their rising from the lower class. The castes are in this way discriminated against by the law. They are poor, dependent on others for their existence, and without an education that could help them. They are forced to wear the stain of their origin. Under these handicaps, they should be dejected in spirit, slaves to over-powering passions natural to their fiery nature and robust constitutions. It is no wonder that they commit many sins and crimes. It is even more a wonder that their sins and crimes are not more numerous, and that many of this caste have good customs in spite of their disadvantages.

DOCUMENT 2

THE POSITION OF THE INDIANS *JOEL ROBERTS POINSETT –*
An American consul in Mexico in 1829

But what more particularly distinguishes the condition of the people in
the Spanish Colonies is the character of the labouring classes. That portion
of America conquered by Spain was inhabited by a people in a high state
of civilization for the age in which they lived. The higher classes fell a
sacrifice to the cruelty and rapacity of their Conquerors, and the common
people were reduced to a state of the most abject slavery. The existence
of this degraded race had a singular effect upon the character of the
Spanish Settler. The poorest white man scorned to be placed on a level
with the unfortunate Indian. His colour enobled him, and Spaniards and
their descendants would have perished rather than degrade their caste in
America by working in the field, or by following any other laborious
occupation in which the Indians are habitually employed. They are
laborious, patient and submissive, but are lamentably ignorant. They are
emerging slowly from the wretched state to which they have been
reduced; but they must be educated and released from the gross super-
stition under which they now labour before they can be expected to feel
an interest in public affairs. The only political feeling which these people
now possess is a bitter hatred of the Spaniards or *Gachupines* as they call
them, a hatred which has never ceased to exist, and which has been kept
alive both by tradition and by constantly recurring instances of cruelty
and oppression.

DOCUMENT 3

RELATIONS BETWEEN RACES *Manuel Abad y Queipo describes*
how the Castes and the Indians feel towards the Creoles (referred to as
the first class) and the Spanish government

In this state of affairs, what interest could possibly unite these two classes
to the first class, and unite all three of them to the laws and the
government? The first class has the utmost interest in observance of the
laws that protect their lives, honour, land and property against the
assaults of the envious and the miserable. But the other two classes,
without property or honour or any reason to be envied or assaulted by
anyone, what have the laws to do with them? All the laws do is set forth
the penalties for their crimes. What affection and gratitude could they
have for the ministers of the law who use their authority only to send

them to jail or the stocks or the gallows? What ties could bind these classes to the government when they have so little evidence of its intent to protect them?

DOCUMENT 4

BOLIVAR'S EARLY LIFE   *Bolivar himself describes the effect of his early life and of his marriage on his later career*

Listen to this: an orphan and rich at the age of sixteen, I went to Europe after having visited Mexico and Havana: it was then, in Madrid, I fell in love and married the niece of the old Marquis del Toro, Teresa Toro y Alaiza: I returned from Europe to Caracas in 1801 with my wife and I assure you that at the time my head was only filled with the mists of the most ardent love, and not with political ideas, for they had not yet touched my imagination. (Then) my wife died and I, desolated with that premature and unexpected loss, returned to Spain and from Madrid I went to France and then to Italy. At that time I was already taking some interest in public affairs, politics interested me . . . I saw the coronation of Napoleon in Paris, in the last month of 1804: that . . . magnificent ceremony filled me with enthusiasm but less because of its pomp than for the sentiments of love that an immense public manifested to the French hero; that free and spontaneous popular movement, stimulated by the glories, the heroic feats of Napoleon, seemed to me to be the ultimate desire of the ultimate ambition of man. The crown that Napoleon placed on his head I considered a miserable Gothic thing; what seemed great to me was the universal acclaim and the interest which his person inspired. This, I confess, made me think of the slavery of my country and the glory that would befit the one who would liberate it; but, how far I was from imagining that such fortune was awaiting me . . . Without the death of my wife I would not have made my second voyage to Europe, and it is probable that in Caracas or San Mateo the ideas that came to me in my travels would not have been born and in America I would not have gained the experience or made that study of the world, of men, and of the things which have served me so well throughout my public career. The death of my wife put me on the road to politics very early.

DOCUMENT 5

BOLIVAR   *DANIEL O'LEARY — A friend of Bolivar who went with him on the crossing of the Andes in 1819*

Bolivar took a great deal of exercise, and I have never known anyone who could endure fatigue so well. After a day's march, enough to exhaust the

most robust man, I have seen him work 5 or 6 hours, or dance as long . . .
Not even the Llaneros (cowboys) excelled him in keenness of vision and
fineness of ear. He was an expert in the handling of arms and a most skill-
ful and daring of horsemen, though rather awkward looking on horseback.
He was so loyal and gentlemanly that he would not allow others to be
discussed unfavourably in his presence. Trustful to an extreme, if he
discovered deceit or betrayal he never forgave the one who had abused
his confidence.

His generosity was really extraordinary. Not only would he give away
whatever he had, but he would also run into debt to help others. Prodigal
with what was his, he was almost miserly with public funds. At times he
may have inclined his ear to praise but flattery angered him.

He had the gift of persuasion and was able to inspire confidence in
others. To these qualities are largely due the astounding triumphs
achieved by him.

DOCUMENT 6

GOVERNMENT FROM SPAIN   *MIGUEL RAMOS ARIZPE – A*
*Mexican Priest writing in 1812, here complaining of the dishonesty of
many officials*

Miserable provinces! I do not wish to name names; I know what all the
provinces have experienced. I wish only to call Your Majesty's attention
to how much a great and absolute authority appeals to vanity, and to
how greatly the bounteous wealth of America tempts even a virtuous
official. These positions are normally obtained by bribery and chicanery.
To obtain the title of governor for five years, a soldier goes into debt for
fifty. He sails for America, not as a company captain or a lieutenant
colonel, but with all the splendor befitting a governor; when he finally
takes office, and before he has hardly time to discover that his salary
does not meet the cost of living, he receives the bills in the mail for the
expenses he has incurred in obtaining the position and in making the long
journey.

What can he do? The more honorable he is, the greater are his troubles.
Because of his heavy debts he looks unhappy — a fact which does not
escape the attention of those around him. Thus some intriguers find out
how much his debts are and take advantage of the first occasion to make
him a gift of money. Now the governor has lost his liberty; now justice is
prostituted. The favorites make justice the blind instrument of their
passions and aims. Requests for the payment of his debts again arrive and
while his debts mount the governor remembers that he has a family and
his tenure in office ends in five years. While meeting his debts he must

maintain himself with decency, send more money to court to assure his promotion, and save thousands of pesos for his old age. Given these needs, and the fact that his salary barely permits him to exist, what would one expect the character of his government to be?

DOCUMENT 7

GOVERNMENT FROM SPAIN   *ALEXANDER VON HUMBOLDT – who travelled widely in Latin America in the early 1800s, here describes the feelings of the Creoles to the Spanish government officials*

The government, suspicious of the Creoles, bestows the great places exclusively on the natives of Old Spain. For some years back they have disposed at Madrid even of the most trifling employments in the administration of the customs and the tobacco revenue. The result has been a jealous and perpetual hatred between the Chapetons and the Creoles. The most miserable European, without education, and without intellectual cultivation, thinks himself superior to the whites born in the new continent.

The natives prefer the denomination of *Americans* to that of Creoles. Since the peace of Versailles, and, in particular, since the year 1789, we frequently hear proudly declared, 'I am not a *Spaniard*, I am an *American!*' words which betray the workings of a long resentment. In the eye of law every white Creole is a Spaniard; but the abuse of the laws, the false measures of the colonial government, the example of the United States of America, and the influence of the opinions of the age, have relaxed the ties which formerly united more closely the Spanish Creoles to the European Spaniards.

DOCUMENT 8

THE COLONIAL COMMERCIAL SYSTEM (1)   *MIGUEL RAMOS ARIZPE – describing how prices were kept high by the Spanish system of trading with her colonies*

Although the mercantile system has enriched a few persons, it has impoverished and left in misery the rest of the population; it has been a terrible and cruel whip that has lashed the American people. Veracruz is the only free port for the entire kingdom of New Spain and the vast region of the Internal Provinces; in that port all the goods from Europe are controlled by a monopoly. Spanish merchants buy these goods in Cadiz from foreigners. They are resold in Veracruz, and successively in Mexico City, Queretaro, Zacatecas, and at the fair in Saltillo. Finally, after being transported some 2,000 miles from Veracruz, they are sold in other towns of the Interior Provinces. An *alcabala* has been collected on each sale beginning at Cadiz and ending in the towns of the Interior Provinces. Its collection is inexorable; the poor farmers must pay this tax in Saltillo even if it means parting with the little rice or flour or chickpeas they have reserved for their own food. Moreover, these goods must bear the expense of long transportation by sea and land. All merchants profit – the foreign merchants, those of Cadiz, of Veracruz, of Mexico City, of Saltillo, and even those of the small towns of the Interior Provinces. Only the miserable consumers of the Interior Provinces suffer the burden of all these profits, taxes, and expenses of transportation. Can any of these provinces benefit from a chain of commerce made of such cruel links?

DOCUMENT 9

THE COLONIAL COMMERCIAL SYSTEM (2) *CAPTAIN BASIL HALL – Commander of a British ship which visited South America at the time of the wars (1821–22)*

The commercial system was in strict character with all the rest of this extraordinary mass of misgovernment. The old principle that the colonies existed only for the benefit of the mother country was acted up to completely. The sole objects thought of were to gather into the hands of Spaniards by abstracting the riches of South America; and to take care that the Americans neither supplied themselves with any article which Spain could possibly produce, nor obtained these supplies from any but Spaniards. No South American could own a ship, nor could a cargo be consigned to him; no foreigner was allowed to reside in the country unless born in Spain; and no capital, not Spanish, was permitted in any shape to be employed in the colonies. Orders were given that no foreign vessel, on any pretence whatever, should touch at a South American port. Even ships in distress were not to be received with common hospitality, but were ordered to be seized and the crews imprisoned.

DOCUMENT 10

WAR TO THE DEATH *Part of Bolivar's proclamation (1813)*

Moved by your misfortunes, we have been unable to observe with indifference the afflictions you were forced to experience by the barbarous Spaniards, who have ravished you, plundered you, and brought you death and destruction. They have violated the sacred rights of nations. They have broken the most solemn agreements and treaties. In fact, they have committed every manner of crime, reducing the Republic of Venezuela to the most frightful desolation. Justice therefore demands vengeance, and necessity compels us to exact it.

Any Spaniard who does not, by every active and effective means, work against tyranny in behalf of this just cause, will be considered an enemy and punished; as a traitor to the nation, he will inevitably be shot by a firing squad. On the other hand, a general and absolute amnesty is granted to those who come over to our army with or without their arms, as well as to those who render aid to the good citizens who are endeavouring to throw off the yoke of tyranny . . .

DOCUMENT 11

WAR TO THE DEATH   *MEMOIRS OF DANIEL O'LEARY*

The Spanish have not missed an opportunity to complain bitterly about Bolivar's conduct and have pictured him as a man of bloodthirsty, cruel and vindictive character. Every act of violence authorised by him was provoked by the conduct of the Spanish. They violated treaties, practiced deception contrary to honour and decency, and sacrificed countless victims. Though I sincerely accept the philosophy that teaches us that the path of virtue alone leads to liberty, I must confess with sorrow that we rarely see a people win their independence through virtuous means. In such cases we can excuse up to a certain point those who, prompted by desperation, commit acts of violence contrary to their better natures.

DOCUMENT 12

CROSSING THE ANDES   *DANIEL O'LEARY — Describing the epic crossing of the Andes in 1819*

On the 22nd of June another kind of obstacle was encountered, the gigantic Andes, which were considered impassable in this season. For four days the troops battled with the difficulties of those rugged roads, if craggy precipices merit such a name.

The llaneros contemplated the stupendous heights with wonder and fear, and marvelled that a land so different from theirs could exist. Their surprise grew the more they climbed, with each mountain they climbed; for that which they had taken to be the last summit was but the beginning of another and another even higher, from whose summits still more mountains stretched on, whose peaks seemed to be lost among the ethereal mists of the firmament. Men of the pampas accustomed to cross torrential rivers, to break wild horses and to conquer fierce bulls, crocodiles, and tigers, with their bare hands, now quailed before the aspect of such strange surroundings. Without hope of being able to overcome such extraordinary difficulties, their horses dead with fatigue, they were convinced that only fools would persevere, through climates which dulled their senses and froze their bodies, and the result was that many deserted.

The mules which were carrying arms and ammunition fell beneath the weight of their burdens; few horses survived the five days of marching, and those that died in the forward division obstructed the road and added to the difficulties of the rear guard. It rained incessantly, day and night, and the cold increased in proportion to the ascent. Cold water, to which the troops were unaccustomed, gave them diarrhoea. . .

Even when the peaks of the Andes had been crossed, the way down into Colombia still proved terrible:-

In many places the way was obstructed completely by immense rocks and fallen trees and by declines caused by the continual rains which made the footing dangerous and slippery. The soldiers, who had received four-day rations . . . threw them away and carried only their guns. . . On this day's journey the few horses that had survived perished.

Late that night the army reached the base of Pisba Marsh and camped there; a horrible night, for it was impossible to keep the fires lit since there were no habitations whatsoever in the area and because the incessant rain accompanied by hail and an unceasing icy wind put out, as soon as they were lit, the campfires which they tried to make in the open air.

Since the troops were almost naked and the majority of them were from the burning llanos of Venezuela, it is easier to imagine their cruel sufferings than to describe them. The following day they crossed the marsh itself, a dismal, inhospitable waste, bare of all vegetation because of its altitude. On that day the effect of the frigid and penetrating cold was fatal for many soldiers; in the line of march many fell suddenly ill and died within a few minutes. Whipping was employed with success in some cases to arouse those who collapsed and a cavalry colonel saved himself in this way. . .

One hundred men would have sufficed to destroy the patriot army in the crossing of this march. . .

On the sixth (of July) Anzoategui's division arrived at Socha, the first town (reached in) the province of Tunja. . . The soldiers, on seeing the high crests of the mountains behind them covered with clouds and mists, swore spontaneously to win or die rather than to retreat, for they feared the latter more than the enemy, no matter how formidable they might be. In Socha the army received the solicitous hospitality of the inhabitants of the town and the surrounding countryside. Bread, tobacco, and *chicha,* a drink made with maize and honey, compensated for the pains suffered by the troops. . .

DOCUMENT 13

SAN MARTIN AND BOLIVAR   *In these extracts, we have two very different views of San Martin. The first is from O'LEARY, who, as Bolivar's friend, was perhaps bound not to like San Martin:*

It would be difficult to find two individuals less alike in character than Bolivar and San Martin. Bolivar was frank, candid, passionately devoted to his friends, and generous to his enemies. San Martin was cold, reserved and incapable of pardoning offences or of bestowing favours that did not work to his own advantage.

The second is from CAPTAIN HALL; again, perhaps San Martin's character appealed more to an Englishman:

He (San Martin) is a tall, erect, well proportioned, handsome man. . . he is thoroughly well bred and unaffectedly simple in his manners. There was nothing showy or ingenious in his discourse, and he certainly seemed, at all times, perfectly in earnest. . . In conversation he went at once to the strong points of the topic, disdaining as it were to trifle with its minor parts. He listened earnestly and replied with distinctness and fairness.

DOCUMENT 14

ECONOMIC RUIN AFTER THE WARS   *CHARLES MILNER – A British Consul in Peru in the 1820's describing the effect of the wars on Peru*

Unfortunately this favourable picture can no longer be drawn, as the horrors which have attended the struggle for independence have so obscured the horizon that a glimmering only is seen of the bright prospect which may await Peru. At present on whatever point it may be viewed the scene is dismal, and the appearance such as if the country had just suffered from one of those dreadful earthquakes which lay all in ruin and devastation. The lands are waste, edifices to be rebuilt, the population diminished, the government unstable, just laws to be established, new capitals to be raised, and tranquillity to be secured.

The late disastrous wars have further diminished the already scanty population; and mining, which displayed some advancement to industry, and formed the productive wealth of the country, has been checked in its operations. . . by the want of capital, by the destruction of machinery, and by the enlistment of the miners in the army. The ruin of many rich families, the emigration of others, and the long suffering of the people from the late continual wars, have occasioned so much poverty and such extensive desolation to the country, that commerce was only likely to thrive by the creation and prudent application of new capital.

DOCUMENT 15

POST-WAR TRADE WITH BRITAIN   *HENRY WOOD – British Consul in Colombia in the 1820s*

England at present supplies a larger proportion of the goods consumed here than any other country. These goods consist principally of woollen and cotton manufactures. . . and a great variety of other articles, together with glass, china and hardware.

CHARLES MILNER RICKETTS – Consul in 1826

The Peruvians have certainly acquired a taste for the commodities of Great Britain and prefer them to those imported from France and other parts of Europe. The diversity of climate causes among all classes of people a want of most of the manufactured goods of England; the principal houses are supplied with English glass, brass ornaments, chintz and other hangings, plate, earthenware, kitchen utensils, knives, forks etc.; the better class of females though still using in the daytime the *saya* and *manto,* adopt in evening parties the English dress; English mechanics, carpenters, cabinet makers, blacksmiths, watchmakers, etc., meet with ready employment; and many establishments, such as a pottery or manufactory of common earthenware, would prove very advantageous.

DOCUMENT 16

POST WAR CONDITION OF THE PEASANTRY   *CAPTAIN HALL – showing how the Creoles benefited most and how the Indians may well have preferred the protection of the king of Spain*

Our curiosity was naturally directed towards politics, and knowing that we should eventually have ample opportunities of learning the state of political feeling in the upper classes, we occupied ourselves in ascertaining the sentiments of the peasantry. At first we were rather disappointed with their calmness and wondered to hear them speaking with so little enthusiasm, and in terms so little vindictive of the Spaniards, while we remarked that the upper classes in the same town (Valparaiso) filled with animation when the subject was mentioned. . . in Chile while the peasant remains nearly as before, his superior has gained many advantages.

DOCUMENT 17

POST WAR CONDITION OF THE PEASANTRY   *JOEL POINSETT*
describing the condition of the Mexican Indians, after the wars

At present se¨en eighths of the population live in wretched hovels
destitute of u⌐e most ordinary conveniences. Their only furniture a few
coarse mats ɔ sit and sleep on, their food indian corn, pepper and pulse,
and their clothing miserably coarse and scanty. It is not that the low
price of labour prevents them from earning a more comfortable
subsistance in spite of the numerous festivals in each year, but they either
gamble away their money, or employ it in pageants of the catholic church.

ACKNOWLEDGEMENTS

The Mansell Collection pages 3, 5, 7, 8, 11; Radio Times
Hulton Picture Library pages 4 (both pictures), 12, 16
(bottom), 17; Mary Evans Picture Library pages 6, 13, 15, 16
(top), 19; United Press International (UK) Ltd pages 20, 21;
Organisation of American States page 14 (top); Giraudon
page 9; Camara del Senada de la Republica de Venezuela page
14 (bottom); National Bibliotek, Vienna, page 11.